MADE IN THE U.S.A.

JELLY BEANS

From Start to Finish

Claire Kreger

**Photographs by
Patrick Carney**

BLACKBIRCH®
PRESS

THOMSON

™

GALE

San Diego • Detroit • New York • San Francisco • Cleveland • New Haven, Conn. • Waterville, Maine • London • Munich

THOMSON

GALE

For more information, contact
The Gale Group, Inc.
27500 Drake Rd.
Farmington Hills, MI 48331-3535
Or you can visit our Internet site at http://www.gale.com

Photo Credits: Cover, all photos © Patrick Carney; page 14, 15 © Rowland Family Library; page 15 © White House Photo; page 31 © Jelly Belly Collection of Art.

LIBRARY OF CONGRESS CATALOGING-IN-PUBLICATION DATA

Kreger, Claire, 1973-
  Jelly beans : from start to finish / by Claire Kreger ; photographs by Patrick Carney.
      p. cm. — (Made in the USA series)
  Summary: Looks at how the candy Jelly Belly is made, including adding sugars, coloring, and packaging.
  Includes index.
  ISBN 1-56711-477-6 (hardback : alk. paper)
  1. Candy—Juvenile literature. 2. Jelly beans—Juvenile literature.
  [1. Jelly beans. 2. Candy.] I. Carney, Patrick, ill. II. Title. III. Series.
  TX792 .K74 2003
  641.8′53—dc21
                                                    2002005757

Printed in China
10 9 8 7 6 5 4 3 2 1

Contents

Acknowledgements
I'd like to dedicate this book to my father, Paul Kreger, for all of his love and support over the years. I'd also like to thank Rob Sims for taking this trip with me. Finally, I wish my mother sweet dreams.

Special Thanks
Thank you to the kind people of Jelly Belly Candy Company for making this book possible and to Patrick Carney for taking such fantastic photos.

Jelly beans are one of the most popular candies in the world. Approximately 14 billion Jelly Belly® jelly beans are eaten worldwide each year! Kids and adults alike love to snack on these tiny treats. Jelly beans are most popular at Easter, when millions of people throughout the United States give and receive baskets full of candy.

Right: *Jelly Belly beans are the most popular gourmet jelly beans in the world.*

3

The Jelly Belly tour bus

Jelly beans were not always so popular in America. It wasn't even until the late 1800s that jelly beans were made in the United States! Candy makers combined the soft gooey center of a candy called Turkish delights with a softer version of the hard candy shell on Jordan almonds to create this delicious little snack.

But how are jelly beans made today?

A Gourmet Bean

Jelly Belly Candy Company created the first gourmet jelly beans in 1976. There were only eight varieties back then—Very Cherry, Root Beer, Cream Soda, Tangerine, Green Apple, Lemon, Licorice, and Grape. Today, there are 50 official flavors! What makes Jelly Belly beans different from ordinary jelly beans is that each one is flavored inside and out. Jelly Belly beans were also the first to be sold in individual flavors—there is even a menu to choose from!

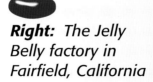

Right: *The Jelly Belly factory in Fairfield, California*

5

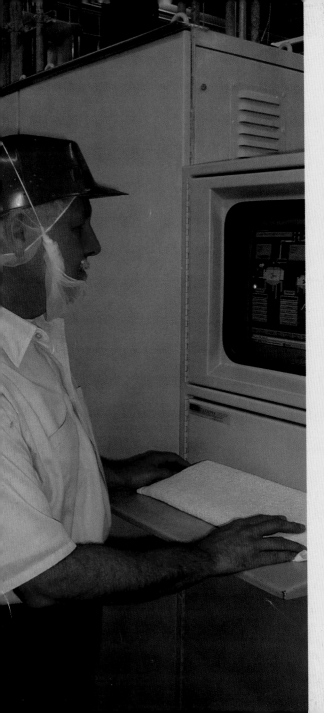

A Slurry of Flavor

It takes seven to ten days to produce the perfect Jelly Belly jelly bean! A master confectioner closely monitors each step. The recipes for all Jelly Belly bean flavors are stored in a computer in the candy kitchen. A candy cook types in the jelly bean flavor that is to be made. The computer makes sure the ingredients are released, in the right amounts, into the candy kettle.

Water, cornstarch, corn syrup, and sugar are blended together to make the jelly bean's soft center. This mixture, called "slurry," is cooked in huge candy kettles.

Left: *The master confectioner types the name of the flavor that will be made.*
Opposite: *Slurry is blended in a candy kettle.*
Inset: *A cook checks the color of the slurry.*

Depending on which flavor is being made, the cook adds fruit purees, real milk chocolate, or other ingredients. The cook also mixes dyed syrups to add color to the slurry. Once the perfect flavor is achieved, the hot liquid candy is ready for the next step.

Shape Up!

The hot candy mixture travels through pipes from the candy kitchen into a machine called a mogul. A shallow wooden tray filled with cornstarch passes under a metal moldboard. The mogul presses the moldboard into the cornstarch to create bean-shaped impressions, or molds.

The mogul then pours 25 quarts of hot slurry per minute into the molds. Each tray holds 1,260 jelly bean centers!

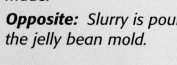

Above: *A worker shovels cornstarch into the mogul.*

Right: *Bean impressions are made.*

Opposite: *Slurry is poured into the jelly bean mold.*

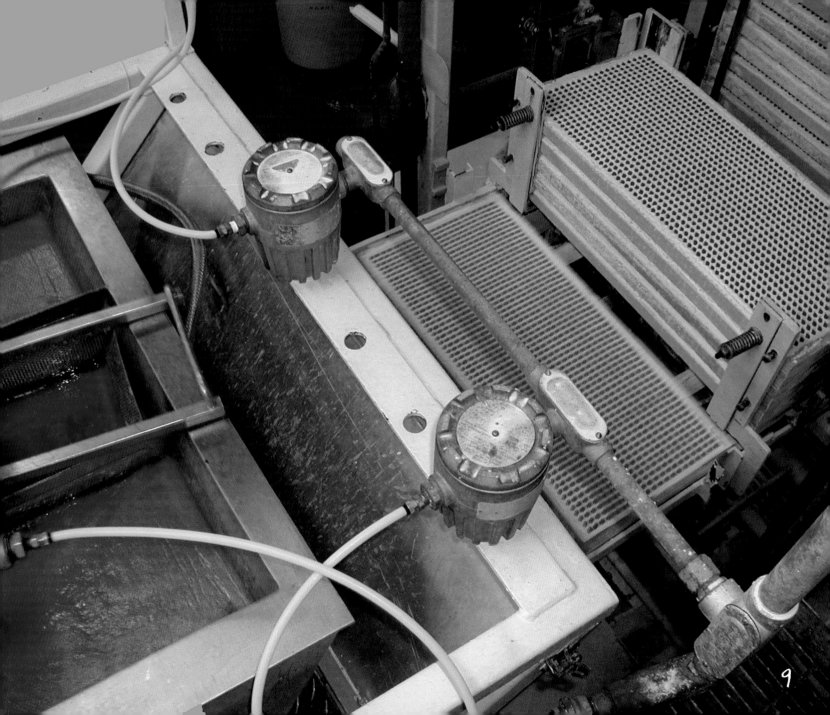

9

Bean Center

Once the liquid jelly bean centers are poured into the wooden trays, they are sent to a dry room to jell, or set. This process takes place in high temperatures, in a room that must have low humidity. The centers rest in the dry room overnight. This step ensures that each bean center jells to the right consistency.

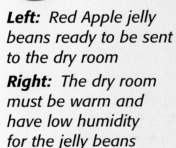

Left: *Red Apple jelly beans ready to be sent to the dry room*

Right: *The dry room must be warm and have low humidity for the jelly beans to set properly.*

Steam Bath and Sugar Shower

After the jelly bean centers have jelled in the dry room, they are warm and soft, and ready for a bath! First, the cornstarch is separated from each bean center. Once the beans are clean, they travel on a mesh conveyor belt under a steam bath. The steam bath dampens the bean centers to prepare them for their next stop—the sugar shower! Jelly bean centers are coated with a thin layer of sugar.

Left: *The sugar shower*

Right: A worker removes jelly bean centers from the sugar shower.

The sugar coating protects the soft centers and prevents them from sticking together. After the sugar shower, the jelly bean centers are once again left to rest overnight. At this point, a master confectioner may taste a random bean to make sure that it is bursting with flavor.

Candy-Making History

In the late 1800s, candy makers Gustav Goelitz and Albert Goelitz immigrated to the United States from Germany. The brothers opened a candy company in Belleville, Illinois. National economic problems in 1893 forced the Goelitz Brothers Candy Company to go out of business, but Albert Goelitz traveled around the United States and continued to sell candy.

Left: Gustav Goelitz (seated, left) and sons

In 1898, Gustav's sons, Adolph, Herman, and Gustav Jr., continued the candy-making tradition of the Goelitz family. Their best-selling candy? Candy corn! With the Kelley family, they established the Goelitz Confectionery Company, and moved to North Chicago in 1912. Although the confectionery made licorice, chocolates, and peppermints, the company focused on perfecting butter creams, or mellocremes. Still, candy corn was the Goelitz brothers' biggest seller.

During the 1920s, Herman moved to California and started his own business—the Herman Goelitz Candy Company. Herman continued to produce the famous Goelitz candy corn. His candy

Right: In the 1950s, workers used wooden spoons to stir candy mixture.

Right: *Jelly Belly chairman of the board, Herman Goelitz Rowland*

business was able to survive the Great Depression, sugar rationing during World War II, and a fluctuating demand for candy.

The third generation of the Goelitz family entered the candy-making business when Herman Goelitz Rowland took over the Herman Goelitz Candy Company.

In 1976, Rowland took the advice of David Klein, a candy distributor, to make gourmet jelly beans using natural ingredients. Eight flavors were created that summer. They were given the name Jelly Belly—a name that was inspired by the 1920s blues singer Leadbelly.

Jelly Belly jelly beans became a huge success. Rowland called on his cousin, William Kelley, to help the California company. For the first time in fifty years, the Goelitz family was reunited in the candy-making business. Jelly Belly jelly beans became popular during the 1980 presidential election, when Republican candidate Ronald Reagan was pictured with Jelly Belly jelly beans. Today, Jelly Belly jelly beans are the best-selling gourmet jelly beans on the market.

Right: *Ronald Reagan, Illinois representative Bob McClory, William Kelley, and Herman Goelitz Rowland*

Color and Coat Please!

When the jelly bean centers are finished resting, they are ready to have their colored shells put on—this step is called panning.

FUN FACT

Buttered Popcorn is Jelly Belly's most popular flavor— Jalepeño is their least popular flavor.

Left: Bean centers tumble inside the drums in a process called panning.

16

A worker puts jelly bean centers in a drum.

The first step in panning is a process called engrossing. The beans are placed inside wide, rotating drums. As the drums spin, the bean centers tumble around inside.

An expert candy maker pours sugar and freshly made flavor syrups into the drums, four times over a period of two hours. The candy maker alternates pouring a dry layer of sugar with a wet layer of syrup to build up the jelly bean shell. The drum spins bean centers, sugar, and colored flavor syrups, coating each bean evenly.

Sugar and syrups make up a jelly bean's coat.

Right:
Jelly beans coated with their soft candy shell

The beans are repeatedly checked by hand to make sure that the coating is evenly distributed over all of the bean centers. Once the jelly beans have their flavored color coats on, they are put in trays and stacked on racks to dry and harden overnight.

FUN FACT

Each Jelly Belly bean has four calories and zero fat.

Sugar and Shine

How do Jelly Belly jelly beans get to be so shiny? More syrup! After jelly beans have their shells, they are put inside a huge stainless steel drum—this drum can hold up to 500 pounds of jelly beans! While the nearly finished jelly beans turn in this giant drum, a confectioner pours on a coating of unflavored sugar syrup.

Right: A worker removes shiny beans from the drum.

20

Left: *Unflavored sugar syrup is added for shine.*

Below: *Confectioner's glaze seals in the flavor.*

The sugar syrup brings out the brilliant color of each bean without altering its taste. Next, a candy maker covers the jelly beans with a white confectioner's glaze—this step seals in the sugar and shine of the delicious Jelly Belly gourmet bean!

21

Right: Jelly beans rest between steps.

Below: A worker checks a batch of jelly beans.

Once again, the jelly beans are placed in trays and stacked on racks to rest overnight.

The Perfect Bean

Each jelly bean at the Jelly Belly Candy Company is tested to make sure it is the right shape and size. To do this, the jelly beans are poured into a giant, spinning mesh drum called a bulk packer. If a bean is the wrong shape, it drops out of the bottom of the drum and into a box. The rejected beans are called "Belly Flops," and are only sold in the factory gift shop for a reduced price.

Right: *The jelly bean sorting machine*

A worker inspects the jelly beans.

The rest of the beans travel on a conveyor belt to a worker who inspects each jelly bean for perfection—any bean that does not meet the high Jelly Belly standard is pulled out and put in with the "Belly Flops." Those that pass the test move through pipes to the printing machine.

FUN FACT

About 4.6 billion Jelly Belly beans are eaten every Easter.

Name That Bean!

The printing machine is where each and every jelly bean is stamped with the Jelly Belly name. The beans are dropped into a tray that is filled with little pockets. Only one jelly bean fits in each pocket. The beans pass under a soft roller that prints the words "Jelly Belly" in white food coloring on them. Nearly 21,000 beans pass under the engraving roller per minute!

Above: *"Jelly Belly" is printed on every bean.*

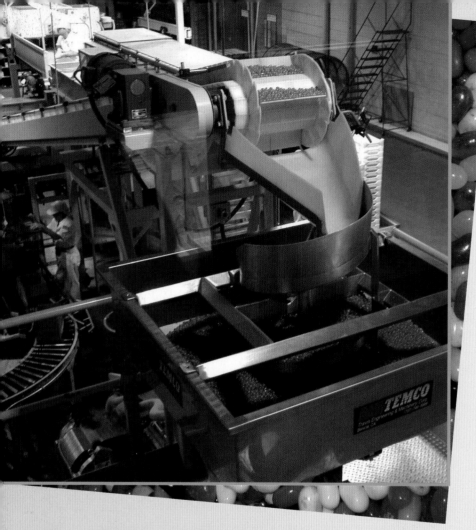

Left: Jelly beans move from station to station on a conveyor belt.
Opposite: Assorted beans ready to be packaged

FUN FACT

Jelly Belly created blueberry flavored jelly beans in 1981 for Ronald Reagan so that he would have red, white, and blue jelly beans at his presidential inauguration.

After the beans are imprinted with their trademark name, they pass through yet another inspection station. Next, they are sent on a conveyor belt to the packaging area.

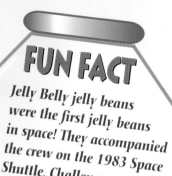

Box Those Beans!

As the Jelly Belly beans move along the conveyor belt, workers fill gift boxes with varieties of beans. The gift boxes are sent on to be put into bigger boxes. The larger boxes travel on a conveyor belt.

Left: Workers fill boxes with jelly beans.

Above: Boxed jelly beans travel to the shipping area.

Right: A worker puts boxes together.

Robots use high-powered suction cups to pick the boxes up and load them onto a pallet. A forklift operator loads the pallet of boxes onto a truck to be shipped all over the world.

Some mixed beans are boxed and stored in the Jelly Belly Candy Company warehouse. There is also specialty packaging for holidays like Christmas and Easter—but gourmet jelly beans are the perfect snack for any time of year!

Left: *Packaged Jelly Belly beans, ready to be shipped*
Above: *The Jelly Belly mascot*

Jelly Bean Mosaics

San Francisco artist Peter Rocha created over 50 mosaics of famous figures, from Joe Montana and Martin Luther King Jr. to Amelia Earhart and Elvis Presley, with Jelly Belly beans. He used at least 10,000 Jelly Belly beans, soaked in clear glue, to create each piece. Rocha sketched the chosen image from a photograph. Then, he painted the sketch, using colors that are also featured by Jelly Belly. Rocha then used chopsticks to carefully place each bean on top of the image to create a stunning likeness of the original photograph.

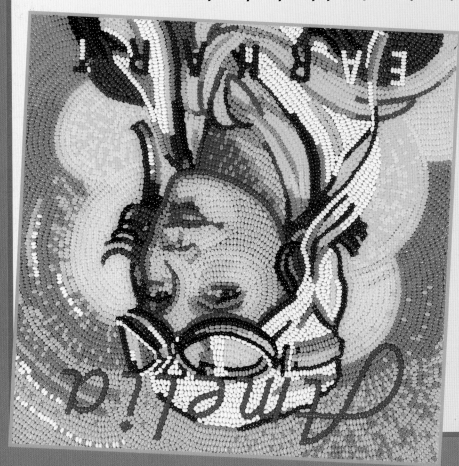

Index

Glossary

Confection A candy made with sugar

Engrossing The process of building the shell on the outside of a jelly bean

Panning The process of jelly bean making in which the beans spin in a drum as a candy maker pours in flavored, colored syrup and sugar.

Puree A thick liquid made of blended fruits

Slurry The mixture of water, cornstarch, sugar, and corn syrup that is cooked to make jelly bean centers.

For More Information

Books

Long, Lorraine, et al. *Jelly Beans and Gummy Things.* Periwinkle Park Educational Productions, 1998.

McMillan, Bruce. *Jelly Beans for Sale.* New York: Scholastic Trade, 1996.

Website

Take a visual tour, shop online, and learn fun facts about these delicious gourmet beans—www.jellybelly.com

J-E-T-S
Jets! Jets! Jets!

Aimee Aryal

Illustrated by Miguel De Angel

with Brad Vinson

www.mascotbooks.com

It was a beautiful fall day in the Big Apple. New York Jets fans from all over the Tri-State area were heading to the stadium for a football game.

Dressed in green and white, Jets fans were excited about seeing their beloved team in action. As fans made their way to the stadium, they cheered, "J-E-T-S, Jets! Jets! Jets!"

Hours before the start of the game, Jets fans began gathering in the parking lot. The smell of good food was in the air as smoke billowed from grills. Jets fans enjoyed lunch and each other's company. Some children, and even some grown-ups, painted their faces green for the game!

Walking through the stadium gates,
Jets fans chanted, "J-E-T-S, Jets!
Jets! Jets!"

The team gathered in the locker room before the game. Players strapped on their pads and dressed in their classic green uniforms. Wearing Jets colors made each player feel honored to be a part of the team's proud history. The coach delivered final instructions and encouraged the team to play their best. The coach hollered, "J-E-T-S, Jets! Jets! Jets!"

It was now time for the New York Jets
to take the field. The announcer called,
"Ladies and gentlemen, please welcome your
New York Jets!" Ready to play, the Jets sprinted
on to the field and were greeted by their loyal
fans. The Jets huddled around the team captains
and cheered, "J-E-T-S, Jets! Jets! Jets!"

It was now time for the coin toss. The team captains met at midfield. The referee flipped a coin high in the air and the visiting team called, "Heads!" The coin landed with the heads side up – the Jets would begin the game by kicking off. The referee reminded the players that it was important to play hard, but also with good sportsmanship. The team captains shook hands and ran back to the sidelines.

Finally, it was time to start the game! The Jets kicker booted the ball down the field. As the ball sailed through the air, the rest of the team ran to the other end of the field. With the game underway, the kicker yelled, "J-E-T-S, Jets! Jets! Jets!"

After the opening kickoff, it was time for the Jets
defense to take the field. Fans rose from their seats
and shouted in support of the defense. One fan led the
crowd in a "DE-FENSE" chant, holding up the letter
"D" in one hand and a picket fence in the other.
With the crowd's encouragement, the Jets defense
broke through and sacked the quarterback!
Fans appreciated the great play and cheered,
"J-E-T-S, Jets! Jets! Jets!"

After the defense did a good job, the Jets offense marched on to the field. With great teamwork, the offense drove down the field. On fourth down, the team was only one yard away from the end zone. The coach gave the quarterback instructions to go for the touchdown, and he shared the play with the rest of the team in the huddle.

"Down! Set! Hike!" yelled the quarterback before handing the ball to the team's running back. With a burst of energy, the running back slammed through the defense and crossed the goal line. TOUCHDOWN! To celebrate, fans chanted, "J-E-T-S, Jets! Jets! Jets!"

As the first half ended, coaches and players made their way back to the locker room. The head coach stopped to answer a few questions from a television reporter before joining the team. Once inside, the coach gave the team instructions for the second half of play.

Meanwhile, Jets fans stretched their legs and picked up snacks and souvenirs at the concession stands. In the concourse, Jets fans cheered, "J-E-T-S, Jets! Jets! Jets!"

Once the second half started, the temperature began
to drop and a chill was in the air. The players played
through the cold conditions. Young Jets fans drank hot
chocolate to help them stay warm. One little fan was
surprised to see herself on the video screen at one
end of the stadium. With the whole stadium watching,
she cheered, "J-E-T-S, Jets! Jets! Jets!"

With only a few ticks of the clock remaining,
the score was tied. The Jets lined up for a
game-winning field goal. The kicker launched the
football toward the goal post. The stadium was
nearly silent as all eyes followed the flight of the ball.

The ball sailed between the goal posts. The kick
was good! The Jets won the football game!
The entire stadium chanted together,
"J-E-T-S, Jets! Jets! Jets!"

To celebrate the thrilling victory, Jets players gave the head coach an unexpected shower! The teams then shook hands and congratulated each other on a good game. As Jets fans left the stadium, they cheered, "J-E-T-S, Jets! Jets! Jets!"

For my little Jets, Anna and Maya; for Conor and
Mackenzie; and for all the Generation Jets Kids Club Members.
Jets! Jets! Jets! ~ Aimee Aryal

For Sue, Ana Milagros, and Angel Miguel ~ Miguel De Angel

Associate Editors: Christopher Pierce and Jessica L. Ciccone

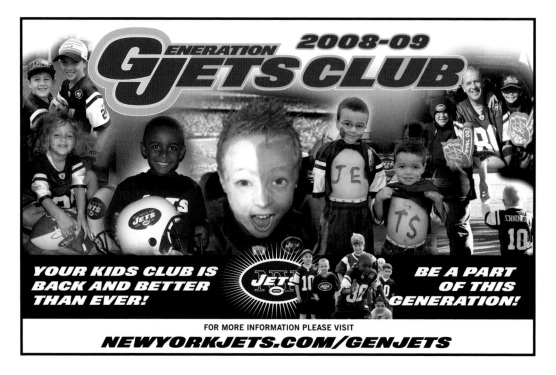

For more information about our products,
please visit us online at www.mascotbooks.com.

Title List

Major League Baseball

Boston Red Sox	Hello, *Wally*!	Jerry Remy
Boston Red Sox	*Wally The Green Monster And His Journey Through Red Sox Nation*!	Jerry Remy
Boston Red Sox	Coast to Coast with *Wally The Green Monster*	Jerry Remy
Boston Red Sox	A Season with *Wally The Green Monster*	Jerry Remy
Colorado Rockies	Hello, *Dinger*!	Aimee Aryal
Detroit Tigers	Hello, *Paws*!	Aimee Aryal
New York Yankees	Let's Go, *Yankees*!	Yogi Berra
New York Yankees	*Yankees Town*	Aimee Aryal
New York Mets	Hello, *Mr. Met*!	Rusty Staub
New York Mets	*Mr. Met* and his Journey Through the Big Apple	Aimee Aryal
St. Louis Cardinals	Hello, *Fredbird*!	Ozzie Smith
Philadelphia Phillies	Hello, *Phillie Phanatic*!	Aimee Aryal
Chicago Cubs	Let's Go, *Cubs*!	Aimee Aryal
Chicago White Sox	Let's Go, *White Sox*!	Aimee Aryal
Cleveland Indians	Hello, *Slider*!	Bob Feller
Seattle Mariners	Hello, *Mariner Moose*!	Aimee Aryal
Washington Nationals	Hello, *Screech*!	Aimee Aryal
Milwaukee Brewers	Hello, *Bernie Brewer*!	Aimee Aryal

College

Alabama	Hello, Big Al!	Aimee Aryal
Alabama	Roll Tide!	Ken Stabler
Alabama	Big Al's Journey Through the Yellowhammer State	Aimee Aryal
Arizona	Hello, Wilbur!	Lute Olson
Arkansas	Hello, Big Red!	Aimee Aryal
Arkansas	Big Red's Journey Through the Razorback State	Aimee Aryal
Auburn	Hello, Aubie!	Aimee Aryal
Auburn	War Eagle!	Pat Dye
Auburn	Aubie's Journey Through the Yellowhammer State	Aimee Aryal
Boston College	Hello, Baldwin!	Aimee Aryal
Brigham Young	Hello, Cosmo!	LaVell Edwards
Cal - Berkeley	Hello, Oski!	Aimee Aryal
Clemson	Hello, Tiger!	Aimee Aryal
Clemson	Tiger's Journey Through the Palmetto State	Aimee Aryal
Colorado	Hello, Ralphie!	Aimee Aryal
Connecticut	Hello, Jonathan!	Aimee Aryal
Duke	Hello, Blue Devil!	Aimee Aryal
Florida	Hello, Albert!	Aimee Aryal
Florida	Albert's Journey Through the Sunshine State	Aimee Aryal
Florida State	Let's Go, 'Noles!	Aimee Aryal
Georgia	Hello, Hairy Dawg!	Aimee Aryal
Georgia	How 'Bout Them Dawgs!	Vince Dooley
Georgia	Hairy Dawg's Journey Through the Peach State	Vince Dooley
Georgia Tech	Hello, Buzz!	Aimee Aryal
Gonzaga	Spike, The Gonzaga Bulldog	Mike Pringle
Illinois	Let's Go, Illini!	Aimee Aryal
Indiana	Let's Go, Hoosiers!	Aimee Aryal
Iowa	Hello, Herky!	Aimee Aryal
Iowa State	Hello, Cy!	Amy DeLashmutt
James Madison	Hello, Duke Dog!	Aimee Aryal
Kansas	Hello, Big Jay!	Aimee Aryal
Kansas State	Hello, Willie!	Dan Walter
Kentucky	Hello, Wildcat!	Aimee Aryal
LSU	Hello, Mike!	Aimee Aryal
LSU	Mike's Journey Through the Bayou State	Aimee Aryal
Maryland	Hello, Testudo!	Aimee Aryal
Michigan	Let's Go, Blue!	Aimee Aryal
Michigan State	Hello, Sparty!	Aimee Aryal
Minnesota	Hello, Goldy!	Aimee Aryal
Mississippi	Hello, Colonel Rebel!	Aimee Aryal

Pro Football

Carolina Panthers	Let's Go, Panthers!	Aimee Aryal
Chicago Bears	Let's Go, Bears!	Aimee Aryal
Dallas Cowboys	How 'Bout Them Cowboys!	Aimee Aryal
Green Bay Packers	Go, Pack, Go!	Aimee Aryal
Kansas City Chiefs	Let's Go, Chiefs!	Aimee Aryal
Minnesota Vikings	Let's Go, Vikings!	Aimee Aryal
New York Giants	Let's Go, Giants!	Aimee Aryal
New York Jets	J-E-T-S! Jets, Jets, Jets!	Aimee Aryal
New England Patriots	Let's Go, Patriots!	Aimee Aryal
Seattle Seahawks	Let's Go, Seahawks!	Aimee Aryal
Washington Redskins	Hail To The Redskins!	Aimee Aryal

Basketball

Dallas Mavericks	Let's Go, Mavs!	Mark Cuban
Boston Celtics	Let's Go, Celtics!	Aimee Aryal

Other

Kentucky Derby	White Diamond Runs For The Roses	Aimee Aryal
Marine Corps Marathon	Run, Miles, Run!	Aimee Aryal
Mississippi State	Hello, Bully!	Aimee Aryal
Missouri	Hello, Truman!	Todd Donoho
Nebraska	Hello, Herbie Husker!	Aimee Aryal
North Carolina	Hello, Rameses!	Aimee Aryal
North Carolina	Rameses' Journey Through the Tar Heel State	Aimee Aryal
North Carolina St.	Hello, Mr. Wuf!	Aimee Aryal
North Carolina St.	Mr. Wuf's Journey Through North Carolina	Aimee Aryal
Notre Dame	Let's Go, Irish!	Aimee Aryal
Ohio State	Hello, Brutus!	Aimee Aryal
Ohio State	Brutus' Journey	Aimee Aryal
Oklahoma	Let's Go, Sooners!	Aimee Aryal
Oklahoma State	Hello, Pistol Pete!	Aimee Aryal
Oregon	Go Ducks!	Aimee Aryal
Oregon State	Hello, Benny the Beaver!	Aimee Aryal
Penn State	Hello, Nittany Lion!	Aimee Aryal
Penn State	We Are Penn State!	Joe Paterno
Purdue	Hello, Purdue Pete!	Aimee Aryal
Rutgers	Hello, Scarlet Knight!	Aimee Aryal
South Carolina	Hello, Cocky!	Aimee Aryal
South Carolina	Cocky's Journey Through the Palmetto State	Aimee Aryal
So. California	Hello, Tommy Trojan!	Aimee Aryal
Syracuse	Hello, Otto!	Aimee Aryal
Tennessee	Hello, Smokey!	Aimee Aryal
Tennessee	Smokey's Journey Through the Volunteer State	Aimee Aryal
Texas	Hello, Hook 'Em!	Aimee Aryal
Texas	Hook 'Em's Journey Through the Lone Star State	Aimee Aryal
Texas A & M	Howdy, Reveille!	Aimee Aryal
Texas A & M	Reveille's Journey Through the Lone Star State	Aimee Aryal
Texas Tech	Hello, Masked Rider!	Aimee Aryal
UCLA	Hello, Joe Bruin!	Aimee Aryal
Virginia	Hello, CavMan!	Aimee Aryal
Virginia Tech	Hello, Hokie Bird!	Aimee Aryal
Virginia Tech	Yea, It's Hokie Game Day!	Frank Beamer
Virginia Tech	Hokie Bird's Journey Through Virginia	Aimee Aryal
Wake Forest	Hello, Demon Deacon!	Aimee Aryal
Washington	Hello, Harry the Husky!	Aimee Aryal
Washington State	Hello, Butch!	Aimee Aryal
West Virginia	Hello, Mountaineer!	Aimee Aryal
Wisconsin	Hello, Bucky!	Aimee Aryal
Wisconsin	Bucky's Journey Through the Badger State	Aimee Aryal

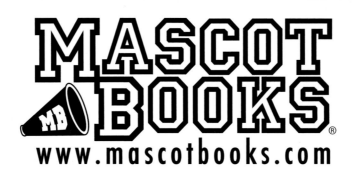
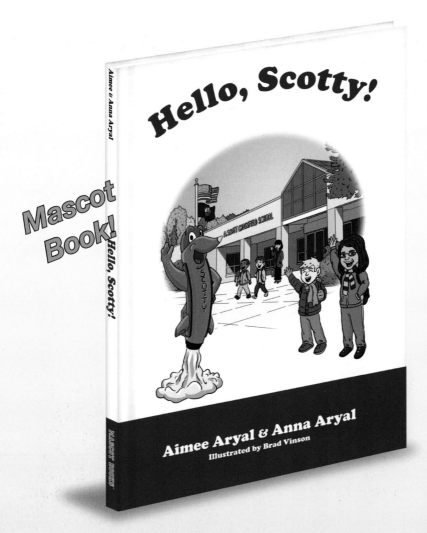